The Pagan House

Richard MacNeill

Teaching the children
learning our roots
from the Source are seeds reborn
and reach into the shadows of mysterious knowledge
and reach above in thankful celebration

While gathering the staff
and sweetgrass of samhuinn
we touch our heritage
where our names, learning, trajectory rise
from the Love everlasting and vibrant

Barefoot in the breeze
these ages are nothing to the ancient stones
from within silently connected, kin vibrating
speaking to each other
amused at the din

and someday the Sun
may melt the rocks
and rivers of lava will be born above ground
unsealing the ancient eggs they hold
and awaiting dragons will be born

There is no need for a bàrd
but to speak from inevitable sight
and leave unfinished the true mystery
of the all-consuming careless need
the Love, the oneness, rising above doubt

Silence takes a moment
to be accepted in our mind
and from them pass antiquity
who swim in the source
as the heightened enjoyment, the right

A father in the mountains
chopping firewood from fallen trees
puts his gloves on a log for the snowy reflection
in a moment's dram from his flask full of whisky
and smoking his pipe: what is more natural?

To bring home warmth to his hearth,
what is more natural? and freedom
a real and miscommunicated commandment
smirks at commands, listens to and recognizes truth
excelling in Life

Good signs of the old ways
a bountiful flock of winter geese
on the first day of the cycle
and snow upon the mountains
where the Mother lays her mantle

It is the time of the Gifting Stag
and up on the rooftop office
the cold-nostril pine-scent
and hearthfire warmth
pervades the late-morning sunrise

The daytime nightingales
each like a leaf on the branches
having been hidden in the summer
are more visible, as a silent raven
flying unobserved

The sounds of children playing
sometimes you have to be removed to hear
and every time I climb into the sphere
there is a toy on the roof
which I smile at and toss down

The kindness of love makes each day a joy
When you spend too much time hiding
you've lost part of the view
the wide-reaching freedom
of open breathing

The rumble of doing house-chores
even writing can't interrupt
and the smell of past days
I don't want to remember
so much learning I had to do on my own

The far-off mountains
the distant home trees
where seasons meet hills and valleys
and adventures
where imagination is true in the memory

and you look around
to see what you can see
and the sky ways are taken by ancient birds
the new kinds are on holiday
many duos on a walk in the sun, only one

I am writing, I'm demanding tranquility
away from mistakes, and hurt, and harm, and rites
where bees fly determinedly
in flowers and heights
searching in joy and finding all of it

The routine of the trapped is not the same
as the routine of the free and living
to work, to jive, to make merry necessity
is the sage beyond goals
who, enlightened, is thriving

Away from machines
to the trees and the rivers
on the water's edge
where life, it is known
on the summits where life, it is shown

The hunting cats, for recreation
stalk wild nooks in suburbia
with houses rarely realizing
how much life they hold
a forest of rooftops in the trees' canopy

To the darkness in your head
denying your intelligence
listen humbly, then banish it fully
Don't let it drag you back
to the years you lacked experience

Make your life poetry
The word poetry disappears
and so this is a must
to live and feast in your tangled peace
so your soul doesn't gather rust

Ah, there is the breeze of solitude
and the yellow birds my brother was singing about
the synchronicity of the happy seekers
Beware of calling yourself righteous
which leads to judging others as beneath you

Learning your way
to release tension for the best days
unworried, gliding, carrying on in the voyage
soaking up what silence you can
so your dream is a joyous portage

Don't time it
don't try to find rhyme where none need exist
Live and be happy
and thank entertainment
smile and relax, don't rush

We must take what time we can
from the indoctrinating servitude
to teach our children our real culture
and not lose touch with our history and language
living in stories true to our spirit

Reclaim your happiness
with family in the old forest
where the sun slants in bright silhouettes
away and near revealed
in the life you are meant to live

A fire in the morning
a calm in the awakened sky
bluer than blue
escape from tracking engagements, from machines
Return to the sacred tides

Wondering where we are
is necessary to remain
establishing a sense of movement and purpose
feeling the source as it flows through our veins
and rectify the ancient melody

The soft winter blue white clouds
sweet trees in the magic forest grow pink and green
and the ashes from our feast
blow in the mind-quieting breeze
and the birds find a higher place to view

My children, you are the other world expressed
You belong, this sky is for you
We belong together in universal tides
and where the Earth, Sea, and Sky forever meet
this fire in our hearth is light in our eyes

The hurtful and careless of others' feelings
will, when we pay attention
make us examine ourselves
and deceased self-righteousness
will lead us to a cool breeze of seeing

Beauty is intelligence, bravery, caring and kindness
a good sense of humor and the will to do right
honesty and the virtue of family, generosity
politeness and consideration, the value of education
respect and strength and the courage of goodness

Calm grey day in simple sounds of home
Go into true meditation, in the Sea of Hope
the center of all - What is hope? It is love, trust
knowing everything works for the best
and the goal is to be Here

Night trees hide the lights which seekers find
I travel these far back dark roads
and find old ways while returning
from schools which look like factory jobs
and feel like banishment

Do not worry about the way others live
Let them enjoy, revel in, feel their existence
and though tired, when your eyes won't sleep
lift up, make the effort to go out in the cold
and be; it is not your duty, but your passion

You owe not a compensation
You arrived here uncalled for
yet trembling, new naked
in Love, the potential of every new breed
find and create your reason for living

and live it bravely!
Yes, dim dangers of the fragile brilliant mind
above the lights of learning on a hill
a wandering lamp, solitary seeker
running dust on the way to the answer; Be merry!

Enjoy, demand nothing
unless it is only the best you can give
the happiness given to you
Think less to inform, more to share
Remember the one rule

The pandemic confronts
all thought-to-be rule
and proves it to be cruel
It is difficult, but a man is who he is
when it's difficult

Are you waiting for it to be easy? You stray
imagining sights and training yourself
to be waiting for ease
Try seizing the easel
and rekindle the time of your choosing

We are more kindred
with the spirits in the trees
than with any machine which lied of our need
and told us to come to where happiness dwells
while deep in the merry moment sought

I should have been merrier, not scarier
and recognized the truth to the cost
No carrier of far-promised wonder
could ever replace or invade, indeed plunder
but only of what we gave and forgot

Love comes first
not understanding
love brings understanding
You are the happiest home, true loves
beautiful sunsets for meaningful sunrises

Put down your hard-won pointlessness
Lift up the mead of the feasting glory
The relayed rejection of life's perfect moment
is a happenstance conundrum ignored
in the right cool sunshine married in the core

I am the Light from within
I am born of Sea, Earth, and Sky
I am
beyond
the stars

I am the king of the oldest religion
before religion
since before gods were deceived by men
the first children of the Mother and Father
who are born of the ancient song

I am the king of the drumbeat heart
of the Universe dancing as Art
The Blessed Blend has its whole in me
the red and the green
the golden Sun and Moonlight clean

Dogs who play as wolves
won't listen to the words of the wolf
but are a mob, a herd
pretending to be dawn
while living a cold death

The dark moon renewing light
floating in pink sunset clouds
and the peace of returning to who you are
after good work
the smell of cooking fires

I return to the old forest
the story of faery in the truth and trees
as so long my mind has been cast asunder
into society's make-believe
which I never cared to plunder

You with your money and desires
me with my invisible spires
grasped by minds educated and not weak
in saying what never has been said
in reading what never has been read

The tingle of binding ties in this indian summer
dissipate anger at yourself and family
your past guilt and pains of wrong
Otherwise, you will become heart-emptying hate
betraying loyalty, drowning in discourse

The lies are most often spoken
by those who won't stop talking
even when there's nothing to say
Truth is simple, truth needs not a single word
to be all of mythology

Summit early, soak up the quiet way
do not forget the promise you've made
happy, healthy, forever in the quays
of fantasy's longing, respect and hearty laughter
from the place you came to where you will go after

Eternal refugees and voyagers' might
sailing from the same through a day and a night
through this place from which we all return
and is but a fleeting glance
where we learn

The heat, the cold, the perfect mixture
thus giving offering of ourselves before scripture
to Ceann Cruach of sight
and the Mother Danu smiling
against wrong to the merrier symphony

Misunderstanding is not your concern
We build the wheel that makes the world turn
we flap our wings to fly above malice
we use our vision to see our relatives
everywhere reaching into Love's palace

If all of us knew the entire Truth
there would be no need to speak, all in couth
no ruth for the supreme in which nature is given
but empathy right in our hearts unriven
from the ancient language yearning to hear

Heaven maintains contact
and helps us keep our sight
on the best
It has been misconstrued
This is all music

A hummingbird hovers
over the soil of our garden work
We'll have flowers for you soon
I know I've never belonged
and I am happy

Some days you are taller
Some days the south is dark
and the north is bright
The wind sings and roars
whether we listen or not

Lavender in the morning sunlight
Contrary with purpose am I
and have always been
The natural, free, eternal
is the realm I tread

Don't let the gripping of stress on your throat
throw you to a land devoid of real thinking
When you find yourself in an oubliette
seek, never ceasing, for the light
and you will find it within yourself

These trees have names before names
as do we in our oldest silent heritage
Does a star need a name?
It shines unique
More than alive, we are living

The clouds beyond color in ships of sailing
dawn, touch the Earth
raise to the Sun
thankful for a day to be
You live in poetry, go

Have you ever heard a troll cry?
It might be the most horrible sound
you will ever hear
The night darkens and black cats guard
the pagan house

The mist on the moon
calls us to listen
Pursue without fear
Beyond yourself
Be who you're meant to be and not otherwise

It takes longer to regain your home
than when you first think of it
It takes knowing where you can put your thoughts
and emotions into work
and breathe the rain-scented spring morning air

It took a leprechaun a year and a day
to return and retrieve his footprint from the cottage
He drank the whisky offering
and left signs of thanks in the oats
while we returned to sight which must be intentional

A goddess of the in between
the beautiful curve of her foot
touching with splashes the mountain pool
smiling among white sunlight waterfalls
surrounded by her nymphs playing on the rocks

I am a tree growing underwater
I am gold glittering in the rhesh
I am a seed floating on the current
a seer of the in between
where morning lasts till evening

Within the waves we were called
as fire by a
far flung sea-witch
to the shores of wisdom's ransom
fire burning within waves

The wild king of nowhere
raging with messages out of time
Climb the trees and barefoot breathe
upon the earth into the sky
and remember, you can fly

Those bored children never alone
are lonely and know not their home
Everywhere you must be free
and live by childhood's chivalry
Reconnect with nature's call

Mornings filled with quiet chirping
surrounded by the silent songs
of books and breakfast waking slow
not tethered to the rush and go
Live to see the day and grow

Returning is wonder from the old, true realm
reader, grab the dreamship's helm
The shadows of seeking are upon us, alive
Blast through the darkness
with your light

All from within lives without
as trees wave to children
who speak with them
Appreciate walks in warm sun and cool breeze
the twilight, the night, the storm, with strong knees

Breathe in, breathe out through the sage
and let it be cleansed
breathe in free of worry
breathe out, shun hurry
and be cleansed in the rain and stars

Walking with my children and wife
on the travelled beaches
in the perfect soft sunlight of home
or along the river's edge, dangerous and fun
we call to each other in the wilderness

I've seen myself alone
all of my life
and now I am learning
to see myself whole
as the burning past wafts away in the breeze

I've spent so long looking far away
I forgot to look here
and as if for the first time appreciating
the beautiful home we've made
where the pines and mornings are in glory

and thus did the King of the Ocean in the Desert
inform his merry band
that it was the last day of pandemic schooling
and they could congregate
and light a fire in the full moon to celebrate

Take the keys from the hook
and make your life still daring
adventure in the trees and brooks
and beaches of seafaring
There is wonder yet to be

You'll get there
Do not hide away
You are a Sun person
Do your silent work
then explode in a manner of meaning

Being intelligent, educated, and brave
is not hubris
Hubris is not knowing who you are
Hubris is over-thought of one's self
forgetful of self-abnegated gifts of the world

I woke in the morning, looked up to the Sun
and wished
I went out in the dark, looked up at the stars
and wished
Now, I thank – and I am present

The autumn clouds are coming
We are functions of the elements
as much as rain and lightning
This is the time of eternal cycle
and it will ever be

This is the only day there ever is

www.ingramcontent.com/pod-product-compliance
Lightning Source LLC
LaVergne TN
LVHW051808080426
835511LV00019B/3439